Praise for *People Problems?*

This book triggers all the right questions, instigates critical thinking, and provides expert advice for leaders that really want to affect the necessary change to enable a thriving organizational culture.

Stan Jewell
CEO Renfro Corporation

People Problems? What a revelation and a validation of old practices, people-first reconstituted. Insightful, poignant and so very on target. A must-read, whether you are a multinational or a small company bursting at the corporate seams. Brad Wolff has a laser focus on what is missing in today's profit-at-all-costs world and with his coaching techniques, leads you down the road to staff well-being.

Claus Schensema
COO Unique Logistics International

Brad does a great job summarizing the true challenges people (and organizations) face every day as a result of culture in the workplace. Brad has created an easy read, with clear callouts and coaching summaries that drive provocative thought about engagement, culture and the impact of our actions on organizational health and results. I recommend this quick read to every people-leader who desires to create a groundswell safe space, and build a focused and intentional team or organization.

Oneka Jefferson-Cornelius
Sr. Director - Change Management, Cox Automotive

In this easy-to-read book, Brad Wolff focuses on the people issues in organizations. Understanding that the future is unpredictable and the external environment emergent and unknowable, he argues convincingly that organizations are at their core a series of complex relationships that must be attended to in a respectful way. He details how to create an organizational culture that fosters relational connectedness and employee satisfaction and leads to adaptability and flexibility.

Combining the insights of neurological research, positive psychology as well as his derived wisdom from working in this field for many years, he specifies how to hire, train and treat employees so that a culture is created that fosters transformational change. I particularly liked his focus on patterns and his coaching on how to change habits.

This is much more than just a theoretical book. It is highly practical, with each chapter ending with a series of questions that invites the reader to look at their deeply-held assumptions about people and organizations. I recommend it highly.

Joseph Melnick, Ph.D.
Founding Editor of Gestalt Review
Co-Chair of the Cape Cod Training Program of the Gestalt International Study Center.

Brad Wolff gets it. The book is well-thought-out and well-written for busy business people. The secret to your organization's success is your people and *People Problems?* helps us see what we need to do to be successful.

Ryan Darby, Ph.D.
Founder, Monday Strong

You want to attract the best talent, retain your talent, create strong engagement and productivity... then I strongly recommend that you read and apply the wise principles that Brad Wolff has provided in this indispensable book.

Glenn Furneaux
Past Human Resources Vice President, Coca-Cola Enterprises
Owner, Atlanta-based HR Consulting Co.

To differentiate your organization requires more than a "better mousetrap" and a quantifiable value proposition. You need an adaptable, dynamic and engaged workforce. Getting there is not easy. It takes leadership and a willingness to reward the desired behaviors. Brad Wolff's book cogently illustrates why the learning enterprise is the foundation to long-term success. It will prompt leaders to implement the cultural changes necessary to transform their organization into an industry leader.

Christopher Drew
Principal, A-R-T & Associates

This book is simply a must-read for anyone in organizational leadership. Brad Wolff provides a clear way to think through the most impactful ways to structure the right culture and environment for a healthy, growth-oriented organization. No matter the size of your organization or the industry you are in, you will benefit from heeding this advice.

Ted Rykoski
Owner/President, Ascent Training, Inc.
Authorized Licensee, Sandler Training®

In *People Problems?*, Brad Wolff provides a clear and compelling recipe for transforming stale cultural norms and gaining a fresh competitive edge. This is an insightful and meaningful look at an area that is often overlooked for its potential to improve productivity and profitability. This is where employees will WANT to work, and those who embrace these principles in their organizations will find they are winning the war of hiring and retaining the best human resources.

Kerry Hendricks
Former Director Finance Business Analytics, Arclin

Brad Wolff offers an insightful analysis of the factors affecting employee engagement and performance with a behavior-based set of practical actions that leaders can take to affect culture and achieve status-quo-breaking results. Workforce Optimization is not just another HR strategy, it's an opportunity for leaders to harness the potential and power of the company's greatest assets: its people. The book offers executive leaders an opportunity to take an honest look in the mirror and determine ways to make positive, productive changes to culture and business results.

Mike Bonsignore
VP – Strategic Initiatives, CKS Packaging, Inc.

People Problems? by Brad Wolff offers an insightful look into the reasons companies today are mired in the bad habits of the past, and what they can do about the people-problem issue. Wolff provides a solid base of examples and solutions that leadership within any company, large or small, can deploy for greater optimization of their teams.

People Problems? goes one step further, providing expert coaching questions for reflection and the beginning of new thinking. At its core, Wolff's new book focuses on the people-component of companies: how best to leverage existing talent while ensuring everyone is in the right seat, doing the right work, for the benefit of all. He provides a pathway to solutions like the Core Values Index™ as functional tools that dramatically resolve people problems in any company.

The Key Points and suggested Coaching Questions provided by Wolff in this book are sound, validated practices. This tightly-crafted book is an important read for all business owners and executives in companies of any size.

Lynn E. Taylor
President and CEO, Taylor Protocols

People Problems?

HOW TO CREATE PEOPLE SOLUTIONS FOR A COMPETITIVE ADVANTAGE

BRAD WOLFF

Dedication

This book is dedicated to everyone, since we're all in this together dealing with the same basic life challenges.

Contents

Acknowledgments

There are too many people who have impacted my life and this book to possibly mention. For practical purposes, I will mention the most obvious ones. My deepest gratitude to:

Behnaz Khodayari, my loving, cherished wife. Her unwavering belief, encouragement, love, trust, and faith in me are a critical part of this work and my life.

My parents, Lou and May Jean Wolff, for creating a family culture that encouraged me to be true to who I am and not to give in to the expectations of our mainstream culture.

Cara Stein for editing, cover design, collaborative advice, encouragement, and publishing.

Jack DeLamater for many years as a business partner and friend, providing support, encouragement, trust and patience, along with editorial comments and suggestions for this book.

Neel Majumdar for suggesting that I write this book. Without his suggestion, it probably would have sat in my list of "someday I'm going to…"

Everyone who provided editorial comments and suggestions (in no particular order): Joe Melnick, Danny Timblin, Lynn Taylor, Cynthia Spradlin, Daryl Conner, Keith Wolff. Their feedback and suggestions were instrumental in this effort, and I am grateful.

Preface

We're all taught the correct way to manage organizations and work with other people. The only problem is that the way we've been taught often doesn't work very well.

We've all learned the same tools, techniques and strategies—not just in school, but also in our culture at large. We've seen them applied across organizations, in all kinds of situations. The people who lead businesses and governments use them. It's the same everywhere, and most people seem to agree that these methods are correct. I know I did.

For much of the first 57 years of my life, I was committed to a "hard-headed, self-righteous" approach—just like I saw in successful people everywhere I looked. I learned it well and applied it diligently. And the more I saw the same approach reflected in leaders and the people around me, the more sure I was of its rightness—and thus, *my* rightness.

Only one thing troubled me: It did not appear that this way of life was working well for me... or for the organizations I was familiar with. Instead, it created dysfunction, unhappiness, and destructive conflict.

I assumed that these conditions and their consequences were a natural part of life—simply the unalterable reality of human existence. I didn't know any other way, and it seemed that most people around me didn't either.

Of course, by believing that this was true, I didn't challenge my beliefs or look for better options. With that mindset, this reality was "locked in" for me and would continue as my reality indefinitely. This is my view of why it is so easy to get stuck in problems and see no way out.

I've always been a little envious of people who have had major "aha moments" or epiphanies that suddenly shifted their lives. That has definitely not been my personal experience, but I remain hopeful of experiencing one before I die. Instead, I've been shaped primarily by my struggles to progress in a manner that's much slower than what I've wanted.

As my process of "waking up" has slowly meandered along, I've learned that many of the things I believed just aren't true. They're simply premises that I accepted from those around me. My beliefs and behavior were almost entirely learned from my cultural conditioning, and I assumed that they were true without giving it much thought. But many of the things I learned were just as untrue (and as widely accepted) as when people believed that the earth is flat and the sun revolves around it.

In the course of this exploration, I've accepted a few basic life principles—principles that continue to arise and determine the outcomes I experience. My experience of life usually comes down to the choices I make in the following three areas:

- My willingness to be aware of and choose the level of control my ego has over me
- My willingness to accept that the true nature of the world is very different than what I perceive it to be
- My willingness to accept that most of my beliefs and behaviors were unconsciously conditioned by outside forces rather than consciously chosen by me

Throughout the vast majority of my life, I have vigorously fought against accepting that these choices are largely responsible for the quality of my life. Fortunately, with the help of countless people and events, I have grudgingly accepted that this is the case. The more willing I become to make conscious choices related to these three areas, the greater my effectiveness, interpersonal relationships and satisfaction.

For example, as I'm increasingly willing to become more aware of my ego and choose not to let it take control, my openness also increases. As my openness increases, my willingness to question my beliefs about people and life expands. As my willingness to question my beliefs expands, my awareness of how much I act unconsciously out of conditioning becomes clearer. My willingness to tolerate the discomfort with any one of the above areas helps my awareness and effectiveness in each of the other areas.

As the light bulb gradually went on for me, I realized that I'm not alone in these experiences. I became increasingly aware that most of my world was also caught in the same prison as me: dysfunctional relationships, unrealized potential, and unhappiness. And, it wasn't the fault of anyone in partic-ular. This was simply the way that we have been conditioned.

All of these people, myself included, were living in a voluntary prison. No outside force was keeping us there, only our own choices. I came to realize that maybe I could play a small but valu-able part in helping people be aware that they can walk out of this prison if they choose to.

Of course, the first step is to realize that we're in a prison. We've been taught many incorrect, imprisoning beliefs, which gain their validity through consensus. If you think this notion is far-fetched, just look at human history for evidence. We all know of countless common beliefs that have since been proven false in the realm of science. Why should our beliefs about ourselves and others be any different?

I believe that the way we've been taught to manage organi-zations and work with other people is just another one of these false beliefs. In this book, I provide my perspective on the tradi-tional way in which organizations are managed. I discuss the problems that result from continuing in this direction—especially in the dramatically different environment of today's world. Then I discuss potential solutions and the benefits of these solutions.

I wrote this book specifically for busy business leaders who don't want to read long books. It's intentionally concise, with a desire to be clear and deliver useful information.

Even though it was not intended for pleasure reading, I invite everyone to receive enjoyment as a free bonus. I also invite readers to send their comments or questions to me at bwolff@peoplemaximizers.com. I am happy to engage in communication that helps create a world that's progressing beyond the challenges we are stuck in today.

Book Bonus: Download the audiobook free!

To say thank you for buying my book, I'd like to give you the Audiobook version 100% free!

You can get it here:
https://peoplemaximizers.com/people_problems_resources/

What if your organization's future is not very bright?

How certain are you that your organization will be successful in the next three to five years? Why do you feel that way? What are your biggest concerns? When I talk to business leaders, I tend to hear real concerns that fall into two categories:

- **The external environment:** This relates to the speed and uncertainty of change in our unpredictable global economy. It includes competition from every direction, changes in technology, shifts in customer behavior, government legislation, healthcare costs, the availability of needed labor, and other things that we are not even aware of.

- **The internal environment:** This relates to people, process, and technology. Often, leaders begin talking about process or technology. Then the topic inevitably shifts to the realm of employee challenges. These obstacles can seem limitless: hiring and retention, productivity and engagement, cooperation and collaboration. Most leaders today realize that their success is closely tied to their workforce, a resource they rarely feel is under control.

Of these two environments, the internal environment is the only one over which we have significant control. That's where the most promising investment of effort and money will be. Greater mastery of our internal environment will also help us succeed in the rapidly changing external environment.

Mastering our internal environment depends on increasing the effectiveness of our people, starting with leadership. Even the best processes and technology will be of minimal use if the people are not performing well. But how can we most effectively increase our people's effectiveness? Which skills will have the highest payoff?

I would argue that the ability to adapt quickly as needs arise is the most valuable skill we can develop at every level of our organizations. After all, if you believe that continuous, rapid and unpredictable changes will be the norm, what other ability could be more important? The ability to be flexible and adapt to changes may be the key to survival and success in the future.

Many leaders in business management use the term "learning organization" to describe this type of culture. A learning organization is a company that facilitates the learning of its members and continuously transforms itself as a result.

As you read this book, you will increase your understanding of how the skill of adaptability can be developed. The conventional belief is that some people are simply more flexible and adaptable than others. Though there may be some truth to this belief, research has shown that we all have the ability to adapt and develop. This ability is based on a combination of individual desire or willingness and a supportive environment. I believe that organizations which prioritize developing an adaptive, learning culture will have a significant competitive edge in the future.

The mindset of capturing a competitive advantage through people is what I refer to as "workforce optimization." The concepts of workforce optimization are old, but not many companies in today's business world practice them. I believe that this practice represents the next frontier in the evolution of business. Workforce optimization is the process of developing people (your workforce) to achieve optimal productivity, profitability, and employee engagement. Through workforce optimization, you can create an increasingly more effective and healthy organization by applying what is already known about human behavior.

This process utilizes years of research in the areas of positive psychology, human potential, and neuroscience as well as the real-world, practical outcomes of organizations that are transforming their results by applying these principles. Workforce optimization is an art and a science that focuses on what works with people, rather than what we wish would work because it wouldn't require us to change.

In reality, organizations have two options available to them:

- Continue to do things the way we were taught in the hope that with more force, discipline and precision, our habitual ways of leading and managing will suddenly break through the hardheaded resistance of our employees
- Apply the lessons that have been learned over the past 50+ years from both research and experience of how people learn and develop

Essentially, we can either choose to work with the realities of human thought, emotions and behavior or continue to fight these realities in the hopes that people will suddenly wake up and morph into a new species. In the end, we can have either the results we desire or the reasons why we fell short. Which would you choose?

Key Points

- Organizations only have control over the choices they make, not the outside world.
- Developing the ability to learn and adapt may be the most important skill for future survival.
- The ability to begin maximizing human potential exists now for those who are ready to do it.

Coaching questions

- How would shifting the majority of your focus from the external to the internal environment benefit your organization?

- What would you do to begin making this shift?
- On a 1-10 scale with 10 being the highest, how would you rate your organization on its ability to learn and adapt?
- What things can you do to improve in this area?

Want to come back to these questions later? Download the Book Bonus bundle to get all the questions, plus summaries of each chapter and the audiobook version of this book—free! You can get it here:

https://peoplemaximizers.com/people_problems_resources/

CHAPTER ONE

We can either change our mindset or suffer the consequences

I t's natural to resist change. Why should your organization adopt workforce optimization over the old, familiar ways of doing things?

The answer is simply that the world is changing too fast. Just as the industrial revolution replaced the agricultural economy, postindustrial society has replaced the industrial revolution. Our focus has shifted from producing goods to creating information and offering services. Business is increasingly competitive, with changes occurring at an accelerating pace. An organization can be on top today and bankrupt tomorrow because of competition and rapid changes.

In order to compete successfully in the current business

climate, businesses must focus on three major elements:
- People
- Processes
- Technology

The reality is that most companies have already invested a significant amount of money, time and effort into improving processes and technology. They've achieved transformational gains by doing so, to the point where further improvements in these areas are likely to yield only incremental gains. That's why it's difficult to achieve a competitive edge by improving processes and technology in today's business environment.

That leaves the third element: **people.** While companies have invested heavily in processes and technology, they haven't invested the time, money and effort needed to even begin to harness the enormous potential that lies dormant in each one of us.

Those organizations that put a sincere focus on their "human-potential resources" stand to gain an enormous edge in our current environment. A focus on traditional "human resources" is not enough. As demographic shifts make it more and more difficult for companies to find the talent they desire, the right people become ever more crucial to a company's success. You've probably heard of "the war for talent," and this challenge is likely to be more pronounced in the future.

It boils down to this: you can hire the right people, or you can develop them. Smart companies will do both. Those that choose to do even better embrace differences in abilities, thought, and viewpoints to create collaboration instead of the conflict that usually emerges.

Those that also work to unleash the enormous potential

that creating collaboration instead of conflict from diversity (differences in abilities, thought and viewpoints) will do even better.

How can I be so sure that these principles really make a difference? All we need to do is look at the companies that have been applying these principles, resulting in huge success and significant competitive advantages. Google is just one example of what's possible when one makes this shift. (We will cover some simple principles that Google applies in this book.) What's even more exciting is that an organization does not have to be large to capitalize on these principles.

The reason that people are the next frontier is that for the most part, companies still manage their workforces much like they have for decades—with a traditional hierarchical management structure. This structure determines the direction of the company and sets the rules, guidelines, rewards, and punishments related to employee behavior and results.

The traditional hierarchical structure typically mirrors the parent-child relationship. We can think of this structure as the traditional way of doing things. Some terms that apply here are top-down, superior-subordinate, and command and control. In essence, power, influence, ideas for improvements, freedom to express opinions, and resolution of differences are heavily weighted in favor of the boss over the subordinates.

Of course, not all hierarchical structures function in this way. Some are collaborative, encourage and reward feedback (including negative feedback), solicit input and opinions to improve things, and have a philosophy of extending autonomy, trust, and respect as a cultural practice. This is not the historical norm, but it is an emerging trend for some of the most successful organizations today.

What I'm specifically referring to is the "traditional hierarchical structure." This structure runs afoul of what's needed for human beings to even start to unleash their potential. It's disempowering. It conditions people to depend upon the hierarchy to think and create, rather than using their own unique abilities that can add to and enrich the organization.

The traditional hierarchical structure also tends to trigger people to focus on surviving and looking good. These concerns stifle human potential and collaboration.

For most organizations that struggle with their results, the first and most important choice is to question how they currently work with their employees.

As human beings, we tend to think and behave in line with the culture in which we were raised. The traditional hierarchical model has thousands of years of habit behind it. It's the traditional way of organizing groups of people, and it's still prevalent in most of today's organizations.

Does this structure appear typical to you? How much does your organization deviate from the above norms? If your organization has shifted away from this model, what have been the results?

Please note that I'm not saying that this traditional system is wrong or immoral. I'm simply saying that it's less effective than other options. It conflicts with what is known from behavioral psychology to maximize the potential that lies within people.

The traditional approach tends to shift people away

from their highest potential (engaged, inspired, creative, focused, committed, honest, high in integrity, resourceful) into a survival mode (fear-based, anxious, depressed, angry, frustrated, resentful). It's important to note that when humans (and other animals) are in a survival mode, a "win-lose" mentality pervades. Others are seen as a threat. Is it any wonder that organizations usually struggle in achieving cooperation and collaboration with their people?

How would you like your employees to show up every day? If you're in a leadership position, you have a tremendous impact based on the choices you make.

Key Points

- Most organizations are still operating from the top-down, command-and-control mindset that was prevalent during the Industrial Revolution.
- The largest competitive edge in today's society will derive from how well organizations work with their people, rather than processes or technology.

Coaching Questions

- Which (if any) of the above structures does your organization operate from?
- What do you see as the positive and negative impacts that this structure has on the results and morale of the organization?
- What changes in structure do you believe would

be helpful and why?

- When you consider people, processes, and technology at your organization, in which of these areas do you see the greatest potential to improve the results and why?

Want more help shifting your mindset? Grab the Book Bonus bundle! It includes these questions so you can come back to them any time. You can get it here:

https://peoplemaximizers.com/people_problems_resources/

CHAPTER TWO

How much time do you spend working in your second job?

Most employees have two jobs, despite having only one job title. The official job is the one for which they are paid. It carries an agreed-upon job title and responsibilities. It's the job that organizations want them to focus on with engagement and commitment.

The second job has no title or official responsibilities but is also paid (often well-paid).This job diverts a large amount of the energy and focus that would be better spent in performing the official job. In this second job, the employee is focused on:

- Managing his/her appearance and image (looking good) while hiding weaknesses and vulnerabilities

- Dealing with negative emotions related to those job duties for which the employee is misaligned
- Engaging in interpersonal conflicts with coworkers, customers, vendors, and others
- Thinking about the challenges he or she brings to work every day from home

The visible behaviors you may observe in the employee related to this second job are too many to list, but they include distracting behaviors such as:

- Non-work-related usage of the internet, email, and cell phone
- Complaining about the company, coworkers, customers, and others
- Overtly hostile conflict and infighting amongst coworkers
- Non-overt, passive-aggressive behaviors towards coworkers and the organization

When you add up potentially productive time and energy lost because of the second job, what does it cost your organization? How much of your people's potential is squandered? How much turnover occurs as a result? What does this do to your company brand from an employee recruitment standpoint?

Examples of cultural shifts that some of the most successful organizations are embracing include the following:

- Developing a culture where people can be themselves, expressing opinions and ideas openly even when they contradict organizational leadership or are negative in nature
- Executives admitting to mistakes and weaknesses and being open about not having all the answers

- Valuing and even encouraging differences and diversity of thought, culture, and styles

As you read this list, you may have some strong reactions. Common concerns include:

- Worry that "the inmates will start running the prison"
- Fear that people will lose respect for their leaders if they show any sign of weakness
- Concern that allowing all these different viewpoints is simply not practical as a business strategy

Don't worry, I'm not suggesting that we implement daily group hugs and start singing Kumbaya! I'm talking about cultural shifts that work—the same strategies that many of the most successful companies are doing, simply because they're good business decisions. These deliberate, consciously chosen cultural shifts can lead to significant improvements in results. They're effective because they're consistent with human psychology.

Very simply, the traditional work culture causes people to feel unsafe to express who they truly are. This often includes aspects of their personalities, abilities, vulnerabilities, perspectives, and values. Enormous energy is wasted in the attempt to hide these "flaws" and compensate for them.

Additionally, the lack of appreciation and acceptance for individual uniqueness often creates disharmony. As a result, people often react by engaging in dysfunctional behaviors like the ones listed above. These behaviors reduce employee engagement, productivity, and fulfillment. In the process, they damage the success of their organizations.

Management frequently attempts to address these "second job" behaviors rather than the underlying causes. Interestingly, management often exhibits these same behaviors that they wish to stop in their subordinates.

As the undesired behaviors continue, morale spirals down. It's critical to recognize that attempting to stop these behaviors through mandates, consequences, and other tactics is not effective and often exacerbates the problems. Instead, addressing the cultural causes of these behaviors is the most practical way to achieve the desired results. This requires the willingness to truly accept a reality of human beings that most of us would prefer to avoid: the presence of negative emotions.

Humans are emotional creatures. We all bring our emotional selves everywhere we go, including to work. Telling people that they cannot express their negative emotions at work drives these emotions underground, only to resurface in the second job, rather than the official job where they could be expressed, acknowledged, and addressed - things that can lead to personal and professional growth that benefit the organization.

Companies that practice workforce optimization realize this and encourage the "whole person" to come out and express their inner world of emotions, opinions, concerns, and fears. If these things are there anyway, why not know what they are? When the whole or real person is accepted, the focus and energy that had been going into the second job are now freed up to be used in the official job. This is the place where you want your people to go.

The greatest recruiting tool you can ever have is a great culture. With a great culture, your employees truly want to come to work on a regular basis. They are engaged, inspired, tuned into what they are doing, and optimistic about the future.

This positive energy about the special place they work gets communicated through their networks of influence, many of whom they don't even know. This is the type of organization we can create if we are willing to let go of our past conditioning and choose to work in alignment with the realities of human psychology. In the next chapter, we'll learn about some basic principles for how to do this—including a few that Google applies to get a competitive edge.

Key Points

- People typically exhibit one of two types of work behavior: The "first job" (engaged and productive behavior), and the "second job" (the opposite).
- When people are accepted for who they really are and not encouraged to hide and pretend to be someone different, their focus and energy are drawn to the first job and everyone wins.

Coaching Questions

- In your organization, what percentage of time would you estimate is spent in the first job? What percentage is spent in the second job?
- Why do you believe that this is the case?
- What would you recommend doing to increase first-job and decrease second-job behavior?
- When you consider yourself, how would you answer

the same questions?

- If your organization's culture encouraged people to be more authentic and open, what impact do you believe it would have and why?

Want to minimize the resources people spend on second jobs in your organization? Grab the Book Bonus bundle. It also includes the audiobook version of this book, read by me! You can get it here: https://peoplemaximizers.com/people_problems_resources/

CHAPTER THREE

You don't have to "Google" culture to learn from Google's culture

One well-known example of a great culture is Google. Google receives over two million applicants per year. It's more difficult to get a job at Google than to get accepted at Harvard!

This reputation is reinforced by the experience of their employees. As a result, the "Google Glow" continues. The ability to hire the best talent makes them more successful. This helps them continue to hire the best, and so on, in a virtuous cycle.

Google practices workforce optimization. It's embedded

in their culture because it works. In an article in *Inc. Magazine* dated September 26, 2017 and titled "Google's Top-Notch Culture Boils Down to These 3 Principles," these key principles were credited with Google's cultural success:

- **Mission that matters**—a clear mission and vision statement to motivate and unify employees
- **Transparency of Leaders**—a crucial element to build trust and collaboration
- **Giving everyone a voice**—a perspective that values everyone's opinion and point of view

These are key components of the workforce optimization principles that are elaborated in later chapters.

You may be thinking, *I'm not Google, so what does this have to do with me?* My answer is that you don't need to be Google. You don't need to copy all of their practices, though you may want to consider some of them. Many of the principles they apply can be used by any organization to achieve a competitive edge, regardless of industry.

Also, applying these principles doesn't mean you have to copy the specific practices they use. These principles in general can help you achieve significantly better results in productivity, profitability, and employee engagement. Other benefits include reducing stress and effort while increasing fun and enjoyment.

It doesn't have to be complicated. We're talking about basic human psychology principles here, not advanced technology principles. (Maybe if we called them "human technology" principles instead, more people would be quick to embrace them. In the mad dash to embrace the latest and greatest in technology, companies often ignore the non-technical basics of human behavior.)

What's important is that these principles have been proven. They work. Though many of them may differ from what you've been taught to believe, they are not "wild theories" that some crazy professor dreamed up one day. In the next chapter, we'll talk about the practicality of converting these theories into something that most organizations can actually do.

Key Points

- Google provides a well-known example of a culture that practices the principles of workforce optimization, with great success.
- These principles can be applied by any organization, regardless of size.

Coaching Questions

- To what degree do you feel that your organization applies the three principles practiced by Google?
- If your organization practiced these principles consistently, what impact do you believe it would have and why?
- How practical do you believe it would be for your organization to apply these principles and why?

Want to listen to the audiobook version of this book, read by the author? Download the Book Bonus bundle to get the audiobook edition free! You'll also get summaries of each chapter and all of the coaching questions together in one place for easy reference. You can get it here:

https://peoplemaximizers.com/people_problems_resources/

CHAPTER FOUR

But really, how practical is it for us to change our culture?

You may be wondering how these ideas could be applied in your own organization. How can you start making this shift here and now in your own organization?

The first step is being willing to challenge our own mindsets and habits. You may be thinking, *What mindsets and habits? How do I change them?* These are terrific questions.

At its core, workforce optimization is a process of shifting mindsets and developing new habits in how we view and relate to other people. It requires a willingness to understand how human beings are wired to think and behave—rather than how we would prefer they were wired to think and behave.

This can be difficult to accomplish on our own. As most of us know from experience, it can be quite difficult to see ourselves objectively. It can be even more difficult to acknowledge and admit to the things that are not so flattering. This often explains our desire to focus our improvement efforts on anything but ourselves. After all, things like processes and technology are not so personal, are they?

That's why outside support can really help in these efforts. The benefits and wisdom of seeking outside support include the following:

- Often, we're not consciously aware of how we're negatively impacting our culture.

- When dealing with our habits of thought and behavior, our defenses tend to do an excellent job of keeping us stuck in our current state.

- Even if we are aware of the habits that inhibit our success, we may not know how and where to begin making positive changes.

- Being human, we typically fall back into the inertia of our old habits unless we create an appropriate system of support and accountability to get back on the desired path when we inevitably veer off.

- Anytime we attempt change, obstacles emerge to block our efforts. Support from people skilled in the process of facilitating change can be the key difference between change that is successful and change that fizzles out.

- Leaders who desire change often experience resistance from others in the organization due to accumulated negative interactions. New people from the outside can often "start fresh" in other people's eyes, which can facilitate more openness to change.

In addition, enlisting outside help sends a few messages from the company leadership that can help your workforce be more receptive to change:

- We are sincere and committed to making changes.
- We are open to changing ourselves and not just trying to focus on others changing.

Why is this so important? As you think about whether workforce optimization makes sense and is worth implementing in your company, consider a few of the benefits:

- It requires less work and effort than the traditional way of working with people. This is because we stop constantly fighting the way people actually are. How effective have your past efforts been to get people to act in accordance to your desires?
- It frees people of the tension and stress of trying to hide who they really are. How well has playing the "looking good game" worked for you so far?
- A shift of energy occurs from the second job to the official job that each person in the organization was hired to do.
- It creates a culture that is more productive, profitable, fun, and satisfying than the traditional way that organizations operate.
- It creates a culture based on the realization that business success comes from personal growth and development. As people develop, they become more capable to produce more and increase profitability.
- A culture is created that becomes an effective recruit-

ing tool and competitive edge in the war for talent. Workforce optimization is not:

- Magic or a quick fix
- A cure for everything that ails your organization
- Something we can implement as a "technique" without authenticity
- Successful for perfect people who are committed to looking good and being right

In summary, developing a great culture is not fast or easy. It's certainly not for those who wish to stay in their comfort zones indefinitely. The willingness to be authentic enough to allow our true selves to emerge—weaknesses and all—takes courage. It also takes time, patience, and skillful guidance so that it can become a norm that's encouraged and rewarded.

As in the case of any culture, not everyone will be a fit. People should have the freedom to make that choice for themselves without being judged for their preferences.

How can you create a workforce optimization culture in your organization? The next chapter will talk about the practical steps that you can use in your organization.

Key Points

- Workforce optimization begins with the willingness to challenge our own mindsets and habits concerning the most effective ways to work with other people.
- These habits are so ingrained in most of us that it is difficult to make this shift by ourselves without outside support.
- Once the principles of workforce optimization are

accepted and practiced, the improved culture makes working easier and less stressful, creating a competitive advantage.

Coaching Questions

- On a scale of 1-10 with 10 being the highest, how willing do you believe that the leaders of your organization are to challenge their mindsets and beliefs about how to get the best results with people? Why do you feel this way?
- How much of a difference do you believe it would make if your organization enlisted outside help to change? Why do you feel this way?
- What impact do you feel it would make on your organization to practice the principles of workforce optimization? Why do you feel this way?

Want to come back to these questions later? Download the Book Bonus bundle to get all the questions, plus summaries of each chapter and the audiobook version of this book—free! You can get it here:

https://peoplemaximizers.com/people_problems_resources/

CHAPTER FIVE

Building your competitive advantage:

The seven-step process to optimizing your workforce

Making anything in business repeatable and sustainable requires a process. Processes usually have a specific number of steps. Since the number seven is a lucky number in many cultures, it is only fitting that the process to create a workforce optimization culture has seven steps! Here's the seven-step process for implementing workforce optimization in your organization:

- Aligning roles and responsibilities with employee abilities
- Creating a culture of professional and personal development
- Aligning employees with the mission and vision of the organization

- Aligning roles and responsibilities with the strategies and goals of the organization
- Aligning employees with the culture and values of the organization
- Assessing personal and professional weaknesses/vulnerabilities, starting from the top
- Committing to work on the personal and professional challenges discovered in the assessment process

Let's cover each of the above workforce optimization elements in a little more detail now.

Step 1: Aligning roles and responsibilities with employee abilities

If a significant percentage of an employee's job duties are out of alignment with that person's innate preferences, tendencies, or abilities, you will observe lower work quality, lower job satisfaction, and lower job engagement. The wisdom of this mindset may seem obvious on the surface, yet it's a common issue in most organizations.

How do these misalignments happen? Often, new employees are hired whose innate characteristics simply don't fit the job. Other times, people move into different roles, or job duties change. As misalignments build up over time, they can fade into the woodwork of "how things are." An outside perspective can help in noticing these mismatches.

In general, as job alignment decreases, the behaviors of the "second job" increase. Some common examples of misalignment with preference, tendencies, and abilities include:

- A sales person who is low in assertiveness
- An accountant who is low in detail

- A marketing person who is low in creativity

Aligning roles and responsibilities with employees' innate characteristics and abilities is often referred to as "putting the right people in the right seats." Taking this step will result in considerable increases in productivity and employee satisfaction.

Step 2: Creating a culture of professional and personal development

When was the last time you heard a company boast that its competitive advantage is due to a stagnated workforce? At some level, we all know that a workforce's effectiveness depends on the ability of its employees to improve and develop, both individually and in groups. This is a key element in developing a learning organization, as mentioned in the beginning of this book.

If the need to improve is so obvious, why is it so difficult to accomplish? The answer is as obvious as the need: "Getting people to change!" Even the term "getting people to change" is part of the problem, since it tends to create an image of applying force against resistance. The drawback of this mindset is that when people (leaders included) sense force being applied, they naturally respond with resistance.

As discussed earlier, the traditional approach to organizational leadership and management is a paradigm of using force and control to achieve desired results. As leaders, if what we know best is force and control, then all we are likely to experience in response is resistance from others.

What can we do instead so that we can experience better results with less effort, stress, and frustration? The transformation required is to create an environment where people *want* to change because they perceive it to be for their own benefit. We'll talk in more detail about how to create this kind of atmosphere in chapter 7.

Step 3: Aligning employees with the mission and vision of the organization

This is an area where leaders frequently roll their eyes for any of four reasons:

- There is often no mission or vision statement to begin with.
- Even when they exist, there is often a lack of agreement on what these statements mean.
- There is often a lack of clarity or connection about how each employee fits into the mission and vision of the organization.
- Sometimes the statements do not convey any real inspiration to people, so they lose the desired impact.

Why is this important? Because as human beings, we innately desire meaning in what we do. A simple example will illustrate this. Suppose you're at an outdoor company event in the summer. Temperatures are in the high 90s, and it's humid. Suddenly the CEO of the company announces on the loudspeaker, "Everyone get in line and follow me. We're going for a long walk!" No reason is given for the walk, just orders to do so.

How do you feel about your assignment to walk? How engaged are you?

Now, imagine the same CEO had said, "Everyone, listen. Your children have been locked in a building with no air conditioning, no open windows, and no water. If we don't start walking to the building now, many of them will not survive."

How do you feel about walking now? If you're like most people, you wouldn't just walk—you'd run.

The only difference in the two scenarios is a clear, explicit statement of purpose or mission and how it connects to you personally. As soon as you see that connection, your vision of the future immediately comes into focus.

It's the same in your workforce. Why would the employees of any organization be engaged, committed, energized, or inspired, when all they're told is that they need to carry out their job descriptions? They typically have no real connection to the result, nor are they aware of the importance of what they're doing.

Isn't it interesting when companies ask, "Why aren't our employees engaged?" The more relevant question should be "Why *would* our employees be engaged?"

Having a written mission and vision statement is simply not enough. Do the employees understand it or agree on what it means? Do they find it authentically inspiring or even see the connection to their roles and tasks?

The written statements are only the beginning point of the communication with the employees, not the end. Not surprisingly, as connection with the mission and vision of the company decreases, the undesired behaviors of the "second job" fill the gap. When you show employees how their work contributes to an inspiring mission and vision, you provide the kind of intrinsic motivation that produces extraordinary results.

Step 4: Aligning each employee with the culture and values of the organization

This step addresses another common area where poor alignment goes hand in hand with "second job" behaviors. Common examples of poor alignment between employees and their organization's culture and values include conflicts around:

- Expectations related to work hours, pace, or quality
- Freedom and openness to express opinions, emotions, ideas or concerns that conflict with those of management
- Work-style issues such as casual vs. formal attire, direct communication vs. careful and polite communication, open sharing of information vs. careful control of information
- Standards of proper or ethical behavior

At the end of the day, people bring their personal values and habits with them to work. When the culture and values of the organization conflict with their own values and habits, most employees will blame the organization as the cause of the problem. Most people do not objectively consider that some of their own values and habits may conflict with the type of career and life success they desire.

There can be enormous potential for development when people choose to examine their values and habits. Many times, organizational change efforts can be triggering events that lead people to become more self-aware about ways in which they limit their own potential. When we make the choice to challenge our beliefs, thoughts and actions, significant career development along with personal growth and satisfaction often result. Organizations can realize tremendous gains in the bottom line when their cultures promote and support these choices.

As in virtually every situation in life, some individuals recognize that choosing to make changes in themselves will serve them well. Others choose to stay as they currently are. Those who make the required changes will reap the rewards from their efforts. Either way, the choice is each person's to make.

The way an organization approaches any change effort impacts the degree of resistance or willingness of its people to change and develop. Organizations can choose to approach these efforts in ways that align with the principles of human psychology, or they can choose the traditional, hierarchical mindset of "Here's what we're doing—you can change or leave."

You can probably predict the differences in results between these two options. For those organizations that choose to implement an approach that encourages buy-in and engagement, it's wise to allow people some time to choose their response before drawing conclusions about their fit with the new organizational culture. Change is a process, not a one-time event. Everyone's rate of embracing it will be different.

Step 5: Aligning roles and responsibilities with the strategies and goals of the organization

Once an organization has clarity of mission and vision, it has reached a good starting point to develop effective strategies and goals to fulfill the mission and vision. The important question from this point on is how well do the specific roles and job responsibilities of the employees align with the accomplishment of these strategies and goals?

Roles and responsibilities often become rigid, even though the organization needs flexibility to adapt to the changing landscape of its environment. An example of this would be if a company's strategy for customer service changes from taking inbound telephone calls to online support. In this example, the company may set a goal of going from processing five customer service issues per hour per representative via telephone to processing seven per hour online. The specific job responsibilities of customer service representatives would need to change—perhaps drastically—to align with the new strategy and goal.

It's easy to see how the history and comfort of the current job duties can lead to a bias toward changing things as little as possible. Given this bias, we may choose to only adjust the current duties where we perceive that things have changed and leave the rest as is. This can prevent us from viewing things from a fresh perspective that is not burdened by the past. The net result is that the job responsibilities could drift away from what is most effective and efficient.

It takes a conscious, deliberate effort to avoid this trap in favor of better alignment and results. That's why taking a step back and re-evaluating roles and responsibilities from the perspective of the organization's strategies and goals can be so helpful. Looking at everything from a different perspective can help people see what's happening with fresh eyes, let go of the constraints of "the way we've always done things," and find what will work best, not just what's comfortable and familiar.

Step 6: Assessing personal and professional weaknesses/vulnerabilities, starting from the top

This step is a tough one for all of us normal human beings. That's why we must begin with upper management first. Without an example from leadership showing that it's safe to be open, honest and vulnerable, employees simply become more committed to protecting themselves and looking good.

Why is this so hard? There's one three-letter word that accounts for this basic human challenge: EGO. We all have egos. Our ego is basically our sense of personal and social identity, combined with our sense of self-importance and self-esteem. It's our perception of who we are, along with (and often in conflict with) what we believe others think of us.

Our egos have self-protective mechanisms built in that are designed to protect our identity and position within any group with which we associate. Anything that may challenge how we want to see ourselves—or how we want others to see us—will trigger these self-protective mechanisms called defenses. Anytime we are "defensive," this is what has happened. These principles of human psychology apply as much to the CEO as they do to the lowest level positions.

This pressure can feel greater in the upper levels of an organization, where there's often a higher level of expectation in terms of others' perceptions. People at this level typically feel that they have more to lose by being "just another person." They often feel pressure to have all the answers, see the future, and accurately plan for it in advance. No wonder it's so difficult for the upper-level people in organizations to admit to the weaknesses and vulnerabilities that being human entail! While a healthy ego can be an asset to success, it can also limit our potential because our egos tend to hide our limitations and weaknesses from us. Any limitation that we haven't recognized and accepted will be difficult to get past. Because these limitations and weaknesses still exist but aren't addressed, they can become friction points that drain our energy and focus as we try to hide and compensate for them.

Here's the "dirty little secret" about trying to hide or deny weaknesses or areas in need of development: No matter how we try to hide them, they're obvious to everyone who interacts with us. They're like the bald man who does a comb-over to hide his bald spot. Nobody is fooled; they simply talk about it with others behind his back.

Executive weaknesses are just as obvious to the other employees. They simply talk about these issues behind the executives' backs as they try to cope with them. Few people are willing to directly confront their superiors due to fear of repercussions. The sad part is that everyone loses in this process:

- The executives lose an opportunity for growth and development that would enhance the quality and fulfillment in every area of their lives.
- The organization loses a great deal, both in the dysfunctions that these weaknesses cause and the loss of potential that is there for the taking if the executives were only willing.
- The other employees follow the lead of the executives in hiding weaknesses, since the executives have shown by example that hiding is the cultural norm for the organization.

- The other employees are negatively impacted by these challenges and add time to their second job descriptions as part of coping.

The principles of human psychology and the desire to protect our egos apply as much to the CEO as they do to the lowest-level positions. The unproductive second job—with all of its negative consequences—enters the executive's work reality just as it does in the lower levels. Unfortunately, the negative impact to the organization is even larger due to the executive's greater overall impact.

That's why it's imperative for executives to exhibit the courage and commitment that this honest and open evaluation step requires. Otherwise, there's no way an organization can even glimpse its true potential. It's becoming increasingly crucial for executives to take an honest look in the mirror so that their organizations can remain competitive in the future—a future where this willingness is becoming more and more the norm.

Most who do take this step find it freeing and learn that it's easier than continuing to play the game of self-deception. They find that the trust and respect that this engenders from others lays the groundwork for a positive and productive culture.

Step 7: Committing to work on the personal and professional challenges discovered in the assessment process

A successful move to a workforce optimization culture begins in the hearts and minds of upper management. Without buy-in from the top—starting with the CEO or President—real, lasting changes are unlikely to occur. This is because without the sincere desire and commitment at this level, changes in the culture will be stymied.

For example, suppose a company wants its people to start communicating honestly and openly so that executives receive the accurate and current data that's vital for effective planning and decision-making. If the executives punish people for delivering unfavorable information, the employees will "manage the information" that is delivered so as to avoid disapproval and negative consequences. The sound and current data that upper management said they desired is now effectively cut off. Inaccurate, distorted and "safe" information replaces it. What happens to the quality of planning and decision making as a result?

This is why expressions like "you need to walk the talk" and "your audio and video need to match" exist. People tend to follow the lead of their leaders—that's why they're called leaders.

Thus, any change or workforce optimization effort has to start with upper management setting the example and taking the lead in working on their own professional and personal development. When upper management openly demonstrates this with the other employees, amazing opportunities and potential can emerge. Employees are encouraged to do the same, based on the examples set by their leaders

Being "imperfect" and "needing development" are synonymous with "being human." It applies to everyone in the organization. When the reality that a human being is always a work in progress becomes the accepted truth, then we have accepted truth.

When an organization evolves into a place where people can be themselves; share ideas, concerns, and opinions that are unpopular; and not pretend to be perfect, many benefits result. Here are a few of them:

- As people are encouraged to express who they really are—including areas of vulnerability and challenge—the energy expended to hide faults and to look good is redirected to the official job where it belongs. People become more effective in their work, and the organization benefits from this increased effectiveness.

- The encouragement to express ideas, concerns, and opinions that may be unpopular allows sound, current data related to the organization's challenges and opportunities to flow to decision-makers. Successful planning and decision-making are enhanced. Feedback that is critical to adapt quickly to an ever-changing environment is provided regularly, and results are improved.

- Ideas, inspiration, engagement, and cooperation flow and become the cultural norm as the fear of making mistakes and receiving criticism diminishes. The synergies and momentum that facilitate success invigorate the organization, creating positive feedback loops and positive cycles of growth. Measurable improvements in productivity, profitability, and employee engagement become obvious.

- The effects of these improvements build on each other to dramatically increase engagement. The energy that had been siphoned off to the second job is now available to be used in the official job, where the organization can truly benefit. Now "this is a great place to work" starts becoming the message the employees send. The ability to attract and retain desired talent increases. Another force is added to produce measurable improvements in productivity, profitability, and employee engagement.

Key Points

Here are the 7 basic steps involved in optimizing a workforce:

- Put the right people in the right seats so that their work and abilities match.
- Create a competitive advantage from a culture of professional and personal development.
- Guide employees to understand and care about the mission and vision of the organization, and their roles within it.
- Help employees truly buy into the culture and values of the organization.
- Align roles and responsibilities with the strategies and goals of the organization.
- Starting with upper management, perform an objective, honest, and open assessment of personal and professional weaknesses/vulnerabilities.
- Commit to acknowledging and working on personal and professional challenges, starting with the CEO or president and upper management.

Coaching Questions

- Under what circumstances does your company try to

move hard-working employees with good attitudes into other roles? How well does this work?

- What things could your company start doing to facilitate the development (growth in learning, skills and capabilities) of the employees? What would you see as the plusses and minuses of doing this?

- On a scale of 1-10 with 10 being highest, how would you rate the overall level of understanding and buy-in of employees with the vision and mission of your company? What could you do to improve this rating?

- On a scale of 1-10 with 10 being highest, how would you rate the overall level of employee buy-in with the culture and values of the company? What could you do to improve this rating?

- On a scale of 1-10 with 10 being highest, how would you rate the degree to which the work of the employees aligns with the strategies and goals of the company? How about the degree of awareness that the employees have of how their work aligns? What could you do to improve this rating?

- On a scale of 1-10 with 10 being highest, how would you rate your company executives in the area of open, honest, objective assessment of their own personal and professional weaknesses? What could you do to improve this rating?

Want a handy summary of the 7 steps and these coaching questions, so you can come back to them any time? Download the Book Bonus bundle here:

https://peoplemaximizers.com/people_problems_resources/

CHAPTER SIX

The key to changing our habits

"Habit is stronger than reason."
—George Santayana

The previous chapter focused on the changes that are required to optimize a workforce. In reality, this entire book is about change—positive changes that create dynamic, successful organizations. But as much as we may like these ideas and want the benefits they offer, there's one big obstacle standing in the way: habit. I believe habit may be the single biggest reason that change is so difficult.

In order to understand the power and stubbornness of habits, let's delve a little deeper into human behavioral psychology. Anytime we attempt to change how we behave, we push against the inertia of our current habits of thought and behavior. If replacing less effective habits with more effective ones were easy, most of us would have far fewer bad habits. The expression "Old habits die hard" exists because it's true!

Why is it so hard for us to change? The field of positive psychology and human potential has researched this question and found some answers. Here are a few of the obstacles they've discovered:

- Many of our habits have existed since we were children—plenty of time for them to become deeply ingrained.
- We're often unaware of what events trigger these habits.
- Just as we have a physical immune system, we have a psychological immune system that's designed to make us feel safe and limit our discomfort. We have an unconscious fear that if we did attempt to change a truly limiting habit, something bad would happen as a result. For example, if I didn't interrupt people, they would keep talking and I would forget the point I was going to make.
- There are some benefits to every habit that we have—otherwise, we wouldn't continue them. We're concerned that discontinuing the habit would cause the benefit of the habit to cease. For example, if I stopped smoking, I might gain weight or be stressed out all the time.
- There's very real discomfort and awkwardness when we attempt to replace a negative habit with a new, more effective one. We're not convinced that the benefit is worth the discomfort. Going back to the smok-

ing example, I may say to myself, "Yes, it's better for my health not to smoke, but being overweight and stressed out is bad for my health, too. I'm still better off smoking."

How much do these points ring true for you?

The fact is, even people who tend to be disciplined and have a lot of willpower struggle in breaking bad habits. The explanation for this reality lies in understanding how our brains function. The field of neuroscience has shown that our brains direct our thoughts and behavior through brain wiring. In essence, every thought we have and any action we take is **caused by** specific neurons in our brain "firing together" in a pattern that is unique to that particular thought or action. A slightly different pattern of neuron activation (firing) results in a slightly different thought or behavior.

It's also true that a specific thought or behavior **causes** a related pattern of neurons firing. Thus, if we choose a different thought or behavior, we create a different neural firing pattern. They reinforce each other.

It's important to realize that the more often a specific pattern of neurons is fired, the stronger that particular brain-wiring pattern becomes. With many repetitions, this wiring becomes so strong that it's akin to a well-paved road. This is what a habit is and why it's so difficult to discontinue or break a habit.

Fortunately, we have the ability to choose different ways of thinking and behaving. This capacity allows us to deliberately alter our brain-wiring pattern and thus replace less effective habits with more effective ones.

All of our habits, whether we consider them positive or

negative, have "triggering events."These are specific cues or situations that trigger a specific brain wiring pattern to fire and our related habit to occur. Some common examples of triggering events and habits include the following:

- *Triggering event*—Wake up in the morning
  Habit pattern—Go to the bathroom, then go downstairs and make a pot of coffee
- *Triggering event*—Walk into my office
  Habit pattern—Sit at my desk, check my email and voice mail messages before doing other things
- *Triggering event*—Subordinate says something I don't like
  Habit pattern—I interrupt her before she can finish speaking and tell her that she's wrong without understanding why she said what she said
- *Triggering event*—Receive disturbing information in executives' meeting that an important customer just went to a competitor due to our rigid pricing structure
  Habit pattern—I blame someone else for what happened. In this case, I blame the VP of Sales for not doing a better job in hiring and training salespeople to overcome this pricing challenge

The list goes on and on. Yet, each situation is the same. I am operating based on **automatic, unconscious** habit patterns. They will continue to operate automatically, year after year in the same way, until I create replacement habit patterns and accompanying replacement brain wiring.

When a triggering event occurs, the brain is compelled to do the same thing repeatedly—unless a new brain-wiring pattern is developed and given sufficient repetition and time to become a new habit. In a real sense, we do not "break a habit." We "replace a habit" with a new thought and behavior pattern that becomes supported by the development of new brain wiring.

Here's the good news that makes lasting change a viable reality: As we consciously choose the more effective way of thinking and behaving on a progressively increasing basis, two things happen:

- The new brain-wiring pattern becomes stronger due to continuous firing of the neurons. As this pattern strengthens, the new habit feels increasingly natural.
- The old brain-wiring pattern (bad habit) becomes weaker due to reduced firing of the neurons. The brain is like our muscles: use it or lose it.

Over time, as we continue reinforcing the new habit, it gets easier and easier to practice in place of the old one. This approach of replacing a habit is much easier and more reliable than the method some people use, which is trying to break a habit simply by muscling through with willpower.

Willpower is rarely sustainable in the long term. Research indicates that willpower is a resource that we exhaust during the day as we control our impulses. It becomes increasingly difficult as the day progresses to rely on willpower to stop what we feel compelled to do. Even if we could rely on willpower to constantly check our desires, our enjoyment of life would diminish greatly.

That's why it's more effective to replace a habit than to try to break it directly. While resisting an old habit pattern in favor of a more positive one entails some willpower, it requires much less than simply trying not to do the old habit. What's more, as we practice developing the positive habit, its associated brain wiring becomes stronger and the positive habit gets easier and easier to do. Consequently, we have less of a need to rely on willpower.

With time and practice, the new habit starts to seem natural. At this point, you've achieved your desired result and are set up for transformational improvements.

With this understanding of how habits work, we can help people who want to change do so effectively. But it's still not enough to help the people who lack the desire. How can we encourage the desire to change? That's what we'll talk about in the next chapter.

Key Points

- Creating positive change is dependent upon individuals replacing less effective habits with more effective ones.
- Developing more effective habits is more about creating new brain wiring than about willpower.

Coaching Questions

- In terms of maximum impact on your effectiveness, what would be the first habit you would like to replace and why?
- What benefits did you derive from the old habit, and how can you get similar benefits as you embrace the new habit?
- What small changes can you start doing now to get

this process started?

- Now that you understand the connection between habits and brain wiring, how will you approach your habits differently?

Want a handy summary of how to change your habits? It's in the Book Bonus bundle! You can get it here:

https://peoplemaximizers.com/people_problems_resources/

CHAPTER SEVEN

People change for themselves, not others!

Throughout this book, we've talked about adaptability and a culture of professional and personal development as the foundation of a competitive advantage. At the same time, we know that people resist change, especially if they feel it's being forced upon them. So, in order to get this competitive advantage, a key question to ask ourselves is: how can we create an environment where people *want to* change because they perceive it to be for their own benefit?

The fact is: **people want to change when they can see clear benefits to themselves by trading ineffective habits for more effective ones.** Organizations can start by communicating the specific positive results people can expect to experience by making the desired changes. The benefits of change are usually not obvious to people unless organizational leadership makes them obvious.

It can also be helpful to tie specific rewards to desired behavioral changes. Just realize that the same rewards don't motivate all people equally. For example, some people are more motivated by making an impact on others than by direct rewards to themselves such as money and recognition. If you look at rewards as "one size fits all," you're likely to alienate some of your workforce.

Encouraging the desire or motivation of individuals to change is the first step, but it's not enough to bring about effective change. Desire alone does not overcome one's resistance to change.

Let me use myself as an example to illustrate the perspective of an employee being encouraged to change. The fact that I'm being encouraged to change means that my current behaviors are "not ideal." They will not lead to a promising future in my current organization. Ouch! This feels like another message in the lifelong series of messages I've received that I'm not okay just as I am.

My desire to change does not change my (nor others') natural defensiveness, which we discussed earlier. I still want to look good to others. I still want to deny, defend, or justify my behavior to myself and others when I lapse back into the habits I'm trying to replace. And I will lapse. That's a natural part of the process of creating positive change.

So, we have potential gridlock here. I really want the benefits of changing my habits, but I also want to defend my old habits when they crop up again. I can easily get caught in a loop.

Sound familiar? I believe that this dilemma hampers many an effort to change.

So, how do we break the loop and solve the problem? We create an environment where people are encouraged to openly acknowledge and work on the areas where they struggle. Very few people will let their guard down and open up without a safe environment that encourages this behavior.

As more people acknowledge their areas in need of development (which were usually obvious anyway), it becomes easier for others to do the same. Essentially, it becomes popular to be "imperfect and striving to improve." Equally important, it becomes unpopular to be "perfect and trying to prove it."

As part of this environment, the organization creates deliberate, structured processes with appropriate support, accountability, and rewards to aid people in making this journey. This needs to include an atmosphere of patience and compassion when people become stuck or fall back into their ineffective habits. A sincere understanding of why change is so challenging can help us and others be more open to change. With understanding and compassion, we reduce the judgment that causes defensiveness and resistance.

A culture with these characteristics encourages people to willingly choose the path of increased personal development and effectiveness. As the successes of this approach build momentum, a cultural norm is developed. In this environment, it's more difficult to defend and deny our weaknesses than to admit to them. The organizational culture now encourages the development of greater self-awareness and positive change, which benefits both organizational results and the employees. That's a true win-win.

Though this philosophy may appear far-fetched initially, some organizations consider this to be one of their key competitive edges. Additionally, this approach is consistent with the human psychological desire to "fit in with the crowd." We're creating an environment where being open and honest (rather than defensive) about our perceived weaknesses is what the crowd does. Thus, choosing the open and honest approach becomes easier than the defensive approach. What potential for truly positive change would this culture provide for your organization?

We've now covered the desire to change and the safety to admit to the weaknesses that we want to change. If an organization stops here, it hasn't yet stacked the odds of successful change in its favor. There are two more steps to go: consequences for the choices people make and practical support to help people succeed in their efforts. Let's cover that next.

Effort that is properly rewarded and supported yields success

Since humans are wired to respond to consequences, it's important to build them into your organizational change efforts. The consequences should encourage the desired behaviors (e.g. open acknowledgement of imperfections, committed efforts to improve, providing input to improve things).It's equally important to have negative consequences for undesired behaviors (e.g. hiding weaknesses, defensiveness, lack of willingness to work on challenge areas, lack of input).

As you establish your system of rewards and consequences, consider rewarding sincere effort and not just results achieved. A few examples of rewards for making a strong effort (struggling well) to change include: words of encouragement and appreciation, taking people to lunch, small monetary rewards, and other small tokens of recognition.

This runs counter to the traditional way that we reward people. When was the last time you rewarded a sincere effort that did not (yet!) produce the desired result?

There are several reasons to reward authentic effort:

- The effort and openness that people display is the cause of the positive changes. Therefore, rewarding the effort makes sense.
- People have more control over their efforts than over the actual outcomes.
- The changes in brain wiring that support the development of new habits are gradual and take some time to reach effectiveness (usually months).
- Most people will not continue to make efforts (which are difficult and show limited initial results) unless they experience rewards early on.

But what about results? At the end of the day, results do count. If continuously rewarded effort fails to produce positive change, then it makes sense to re-evaluate both the effort and the rewards.

Still, if an organization truly wants to create a positive, adaptive learning culture, it needs to look beyond employee performance alone. Rewarding top performers who have a negative impact on the culture is common—and usually self-defeating. Most leaders find it difficult to terminate top performers, but it needs to be done when their negative impact on the organization's culture outweighs the positive impacts of their performance.

Below are two actual examples of consequences used by highly successful companies that embrace this philosophy. They have chosen to reward long-term cultural impact, not just current results.

- Performance evaluations are structured to be 50% based on work performance and 50% based on effort and contribution to the company culture.
- Star performers who have a negative effect on the culture and are not willing to change are terminated.

Support to help people make lasting change

Now that we've deliberately encouraged people to choose to make the effort to change, we have one last practical consideration. Most people need the support of others to catch themselves when the old behaviors occur. It takes time to build keen awareness of these old, unconscious habit patterns.

Another reason people need support in making changes is that we need help seeing our blind spots. As we've discussed, it's hard enough making changes that we're aware of and know will benefit us. It's even harder to change something we're not aware of. As in the aforementioned comb-over example, our blind spots are frequently obvious to everyone else. But we don't want to face them, so we often ignore any reference to them or get defensive if they're mentioned.

Yet these areas represent an untapped opportunity if we truly want to live our full potential. How can we overcome our resistance as well as accurately see our blind spots and choose to change them?

As previously mentioned, it helps to have a culture of support founded on the premise that we're all imperfect human beings who are continuously in the process of developing. When we acknowledge this truth and make it the accepted norm, defenses are lowered and people become more open.

In this environment, people can provide honest support and feedback to help us increase our awareness. Once we become aware and face these limiting behaviors, we can make a conscious choice to change or stay the way we are.

In our Western culture, it's common to feel initial resistance to the idea of asking others to help us change. We've been conditioned to believe we should be able to do it ourselves. The truth is that getting the appropriate support in helping us change and grow is not a sign of weakness. It's a sign of a sincere desire to be effective and efficient.

People who commonly provide support in the form of feedback and encouragement at work include trusted co-workers, supervisors, and professional coaching support. There are several reasons why this is the case:

- It's difficult to see ourselves clearly, especially with automatic habit patterns that have been in place for years.
- It's difficult to catch ourselves quickly when we slip back into our old habits—which we will.
- Support in the form of feedback and encouragement from people we trust can go a long way. It makes it easier to increase our awareness and regularly take the actions needed to build more effective habits.

When an organization develops the philosophy and practice of people supporting each other in their development, the increase in collaboration that results creates tremendous synergies. Potentials are unleashed that benefit the individual employees and the organization itself.

This is more than enough reason to take these steps forward. However, there's another benefit to prioritizing the professional and personal development of employees. We move from the realm of incremental change to the realm of transformational change! The difference between these two types of change is monumental. It can mean the difference between going out of business and being an industry leader. I'll explain why in the next chapter.

Key Points

There are 4 basic steps to intentionally bringing about effective and sustainable change:

- Helping people see the benefit to themselves if they choose to change
- Creating a safe environment that encourages people to admit to themselves and others that changing would be a good thing to do
- Creating an appropriate system of rewards and punishments that encourage people to make the effort to change
- Enlisting consistent, practical support of others to help us see our blind spots as well as alert and encourage us when our old habit patterns emerge

Coaching Questions

- Thinking of a positive change effort that would help your company, how can you show the people involved that they'll achieve worthwhile benefits if they change?

- What specific things can you do to create a safe environment for people to admit to weaknesses that they want to change?
- What do you believe would be appropriate positive and negative consequences for people to make the actual effort to change?
- What would help you become aware of blind spots that negatively impact your effectiveness?
- Whom would you feel comfortable asking for feedback in the areas of these blind spots so that you can move closer to your potential?
- How would you prefer to receive feedback from others when you exhibit habits that you've announced you would like to change?

Want to come back to these questions later? Download the Book Bonus bundle to get all the questions, plus summaries of each chapter and the audiobook version of this book—free!

You can get it here:

https://peoplemaximizers.com/people_problems_resources/

CHAPTER EIGHT

Do you want small improvement or transformational improvement?

The answer to this question is obvious: transformational improvement! Surprisingly, the effort involved in transformational improvement is not necessarily greater than for small improvement. Let's take a closer look. Most of the change we're accustomed to is incremental rather than transformational in nature. For example, typical process changes may seek to increase production from 10 widgets per hour to 11 or to reduce defects from 2% to 1%. No doubt these are positive changes and worthy of pursuit, but they're incremental nonetheless.

Transformational changes are exponential in nature—for example, a 500% improvement rather than a 5% improvement. These changes always involve shifts in mindsets and beliefs, rather than simply improvements in processes or technology.

For example, under the prevalent belief in Europe that the Earth is flat, people traveled by ship but stayed close to shore. The widespread acceptance that the Earth is round was a change in belief that transformed mindsets about what is possible. The transformative exploration of the entire world by Europeans was begun with a mindset change, rather than a change in process or technology.

Even what we routinely consider to be technological innovations are not transformative until the associated beliefs and mindsets change. For example, the internet was around for years, but the shift in belief and subsequent mindsets about what could be done with the internet caused the transformations that we experience today.

The focus of workforce optimization is a paradigm shift. The focus shifts from processes and technology (usually incremental change) to the potential of the human mind and human interaction synergies (transformational change).

To illustrate this difference, consider a silly example that shows the difference in impact of a process approach versus working directly on beliefs and mindsets. Let's suppose that I have an intense fear of the Boogeyman. I'm an employee of an organization, and this fear distracts much of my focus while at work. Approximately 50% of my energy is siphoned away while I ruminate, talk about it, and plan tactics for avoiding harm from my imagined enemy. Let's also suppose that I work at a company that values me and desires to work with me to overcome my fear so that I can be a productive employee.

The VP of Human Resources decides to assign an internal coach who applies a very rational process improvement approach to my challenge. My coach works with me to reduce the amount of focus and productivity lost to my fear. Together, we set a goal of reducing this drag on my performance from four hours per day to only three hours per day—a significant 25% improvement.

Over time, I create various processes that really do help. I tap my feet three times. If that doesn't work, I close my eyes and think of butterflies and unicorns. And if *that* doesn't work, I go for a walk and sing my favorite songs.

Eventually, over a six-month period, I meet my goal. We calculate that in a year, this would improve my productivity (assuming 2000 hours in a year) from a loss of 1000 hours per year to a loss of 750 hours per year. If my productivity is estimated to bring the organization $100 per hour, the improvement would benefit the organization by an extra $25,000 per year in productivity.

This is an example of incremental improvement. The process improvement initiative is declared a success—backed up with specific, measurable criteria.

But then, by sheer luck, the VP of Human Resources meets a coach who has an entirely different approach. This coach's approach is to address the root cause of the issue itself, which is almost always in the realm of beliefs and mindsets.

This coach is assigned to me and works with me to challenge my belief that the Boogeyman exists at all. After a month of challenging my belief, I am convinced that since there has never been actual evidence from others or myself, I can safely toss this rascal into the box where Santa Claus and the Tooth Fairy were exiled years before.

Suddenly, with much less time and effort, my productivity issues in this arena are not just improved but solved! Additionally, I bring far more engaged energy to my work and develop better relationships with coworkers, which adds more to the organization than my increased productivity alone.

This is an example of transformational improvement, and its applications go far beyond this simple illustration. Mindsets and beliefs are at the root of more productivity issues than most people realize. That's great news, because these issues represent abundant opportunities for transformational improvements and great leaps forward throughout an organization.

Key Point

- We usually attempt to improve through process improvements, which are incremental. The opportunities for truly transformational change lie in our beliefs and mindsets.

Coaching Questions

- Thinking of a change you would like to make in your company, what would be an incremental improvement approach involving tweaking a process?
- Thinking of the same change, what would be a potentially transformational improvement approach that involves changing your underlying beliefs about the situation? How about changing how you look at the

situation (your mindset)?
- What new possibilities emerged by focusing on the transformational approach?

Want to listen to the audiobook version of this book, read by the author? Download the Book Bonus bundle to get the audiobook edition free! You'll also get summaries of each chapter and all of the coaching questions together in one place for easy reference. You can get it here:

https://peoplemaximizers.com/people_problems_resources/

CHAPTER NINE

What type of future do you foresee for your organization?

I began this book with the question, "What if your organization's future is not very bright?" It seems fitting to conclude the book with a very similar question. Everything discussed relates to choices that leaders of organizations need to make. The evidence suggests that traditional organizational management philosophy poses great risks to future success—and even survival.

I do not believe that anybody can accurately predict the future on a regular basis. However, we can identify major paradigm shifts that create eras that define human history, such as the shift from an agrarian society to the industrial revolution, or the more recent shift to the postindustrial era.

One of the shifts that I find fascinating is the change in the rules of business success. It used to be that it took many years and a large amount of people, capital, and tangible assets to build the most successful companies. Now, with companies like Google, Amazon, and many others, it's more about changing the way we look at things (mindsets) and having people work differently. These companies chose not to accept the pre-existing rules of business or the world that they were taught.

Companies of this type can produce in a few years what would have taken decades to create in prior eras—and with fewer people and far less capital and tangible assets. This suggests that a competitive edge today is related more to unleashing human potential than to having a specific technology, process, or large army of people. The hottest technology or process today can be obsolete tomorrow. Then what?

An organization that focuses on developing a great culture in order to maximize the potential of their people (even if small in number) can continue to learn, adapt, and thrive—even when the technology or processes that gave them a competitive edge no longer do.

Consider how many dominant technologies and companies have gone out of business or become obsolete in the recent past. In many cases, that happened because a small upstart company created a better option. This should give us pause.

As you think about how this might apply to your organization, consider which key elements will provide a competitive advantage in the future. You might even consider whether your organization will be in business in a few years if you continue to think and do things as you do now.

This is why the concept of workforce optimization to create an adaptive, learning organization can be so powerful. This type of organizational culture sees its competitive advantage as the ability to quickly change as challenges and opportunities emerge. It provides the greatest opportunity to survive and thrive in our current world. Specific characteristics of the culture I'm describing include:

- Promoting positive changes, even when it's uncomfortable
- Quickly identifying and changing habits of thought and behavior that are no longer working (even if they worked in the past)
- Willingness of people at the top to be more open to learning and adapting, because they no longer believe that they need to have all the answers
- Dedication from the top down to truth and vulnerability over "hiding" personal weaknesses and always needing to be right
- Encouraging information, ideas, and disagreement from lower levels
- Recognizing mistakes and imperfections as part of the process of innovation and experimentation
- Learning and adapting quickly

When you compare the above characteristics to that of traditional organizational cultures, what stands out for you? If you were placing a bet on which type of culture is more likely to succeed in the future, which side would you bet on?

If you're a leader in an organization, you're placing a bet every day you go to work. The choice is yours to make. What do you choose?

Key Points

- The traditional rules that governed business success have changed significantly since the 1990s. Things happen much faster and require fewer people and less capital.
- Dominant technologies and processes can become obsolete very quickly. An adaptive, learning organizational culture is the most important resource for future success and survival.

Coaching Questions

- What do you see as the greatest threats to the survival of your company in the future?
- How can you begin to apply the concepts of an adaptive, learning organizational culture to address these threats now?

Want a handy summary of each chapter of this book, plus all the coaching questions, so you can come back to them any time? Download the Book Bonus bundle to get it all for easy reference. You can get it here:

https://peoplemaximizers.com/people_problems_resources/

About the author

Brad Wolff is the People Maximizer. He specializes in workforce optimization and guiding companies to make the most of their "human potential resources." His passion is empowering people to create the business success and life fulfillment they desire, in a deep and lasting way.

Brad is Managing Partner for PeopleMax, an Atlanta-based Workforce Optimization firm. Its focus is helping companies gain control over their people problems to increase productivity, profitability and employee engagement while reducing stress and conflict. This encompasses employee alignment, development of a great culture, successful strategy and leadership effectiveness.

A CPA by training, Brad combines his analytical skills with more than 20 years in the recruiting business to achieve success for his clients. He's also a Certified Professional Coach through the Institute for Professional Excellence in Coaching (iPEC). He also has Certification in Managing Change in Human Systems from the Center for Human Systems.

You can contact Brad at bwolff@peoplemaximizers.com.

TURNING PEOPLE PROBLEMS INTO PEOPLE SOLUTIONS:
Thriving in a Changing World

In today's fast-changing, unpredictable world, surviving is difficult. You can have the dominant product or service today and be **obsolete almost overnight.** Those organizations that choose to become **flexible, adaptive, learning organizations,** go beyond surviving to thriving!

Your audience will leave with:
- **A practical 7-step model to implement workforce optimization** to create a flexible, adaptive, learning organization
- Solid evidence from prominent companies that **apply these principles and solutions to old problems they've been stuck in for years**

The keys to workforce optimization that are sitting right under their noses. When they recognize and identify these keys, they'll be on their way to higher profits and productivity!

This program is available as a keynote, seminar, or executive session. Learn more here:
PeopleMaximizers.com/people-solutions

85592806R00055

Made in the USA
Lexington, KY
02 April 2018